MASTER YOUR
TENNIS
GAME

MASTER YOUR
TENNIS
GAME

50 MENTAL STRATEGIES AND TACTICS

KEN DeHART

**ROCKRIDGE
PRESS**

For general information on our other products and services or to obtain technical support, please contact our Customer Care Department within the U.S. at (866) 744-2665, or outside the U.S. at (510) 253-0500.

Rockridge Press publishes its books in a variety of electronic and print formats. Some content that appears in print may not be available in electronic books, and vice versa.

Interior and Cover Designer: Michael Patti
Art Producer: Michael Hardgrove
Editor: Marjorie DeWitt
Production Editor: Andrew Yackira
Production Manager: Holly Haydash
Cover Illustration: So Young Kim
Interior Illustrations: John Jay Cabuay

ISBN: Print 978-1-64152-846-7 | eBook 978-1-64152-847-4
R0

Dedicated to my wife,
Karen, and my son,
Kameron

CONTENTS

Introduction

LOVE FOR THE GAME

As a college freshman, I played basketball and baseball, but I had never seen anyone play tennis. One day I was running by the college tennis courts and saw some other students playing the game. I was intrigued. I went to Kmart and bought my first Wilson Jack Kramer racket and a can of Wilson tennis balls.

Soon I began to hit with my roommate every day. I was hooked! How to hit and move came pretty naturally to me from the other sports I had played growing up. I could never afford tennis lessons, but I learned a lot watching the game being played by others and on television.

I began to watch the college team practice and eventually asked the Campbellsville University tennis coach if I could practice with the men's team. Miss Osborne allowed me to attend practices, clean up the courts, hit with both the men's and women's teams, and travel to the away matches. While we traveled she would explain what was going on tactically and mentally in the matches. My love for the game and desire to play more successfully grew more and more each time I played.

My athletic director at Campbellsville helped me receive an assistantship to attend graduate school at Western Kentucky University in Bowling Green. I taught tennis and other related sports as part of the program to pay for my education, and my knowledge of the game grew even more. My roommates at WKU were all Olympic athletes in other sports, such as shot put, javelin, and the triple jump. We spent hours discussing how all the sports related to each other, training routines, and how to deal with the ups and downs of training and competition.

After graduate school, I became a teacher at Campbellsville High School, where I taught a business-vocational program called Distributive Education. I had participated in this program during my own high school experience. In addition, I coached the boys' tennis team and had a very successful three-year run. My brief but passionate experience as a successful college player and conversations with my Olympic athlete roommates would prove very valuable as a high school coach with athletes who had limited experience as competitive players.

My own game continued to improve as I took a more in-depth approach to understanding the tactical and mental side of tennis. An unexpected opportunity arose for me at a tournament I was competing at in Murray, Kentucky: the chance to interview for the director of tennis position at Sequoia Swim and Tennis Club in Nashville, Tennessee. I was offered the position and subsequently moved from Campbellsville to Nashville. My tennis coaching career was underway.

Now, 50 years later, I have won many tennis titles and coached thousands of players. Along the way, I have found that I love teaching others to play as much as I love playing the game. I attended every tennis teaching course I could to learn more about the game. In fact, I won the USPTA Career Development Award three years in a row for the most continuing education points of any teaching professional in the United States. I truly enjoyed studying under great sports psychologists such as Dr. Jim Loehr and Dr. Allen Fox to better understand how to help players develop mental toughness.

While technique is important, mental discipline and focus are what make an athlete successful. I was fortunate enough to have learned that from my other sports, and it carried over and grew with my tennis game. Physical skills are limited by underdeveloped mental skills. As my mental skills improved, so did my athletic skills and my match play performance. I devised my own course, Defeating the Monsters in Your Mind, which incorporated all aspects of the game. As a tennis teaching professional, I realize the value of total player development in four key areas: technique, tactics, movement, and mental skills. The mental skills allow the successful application of technique, tactics, and movement and help you manage stress, maintain composure in challenging situations, and believe that you can accomplish anything.

Mental skills can include breathing, meditation, and, in general, an awareness of how to use the mind to control the body in sports and in life.

HOW TO BEST USE THIS BOOK

With this book, I hope to show you the essential role that mental skills play in improving your overall tennis game. Depending upon your approach to learning, one way to incorporate the book into practice is to jump to specific chapters that relate to your areas of interest. Or, you may simply read the entire book all at once, making note of certain points for reference. Before you start applying what you've learned in this book to your game, I suggest that you first select key areas you want to improve.

Because I am so emotionally invested in a match, I find it challenging to think logically and use tactics I have at my command. I even take my book to the court for my matches with key points highlighted and review them at the changeovers to keep me focused. This is a strategy that even top tour-level players often do. Serena Williams, for example, has looked at her notes on a changeover during a match.

I congratulate you on taking a proactive step to improving your game tactically and mentally with this book. I am confident that you will experience improvements and a growing awareness of how to use your mental skill to enjoy continued success in your tennis game.

"We're playing a sport. A lot of times players forget it's a game. That's not how it should be; it should be fun."

—ROD LAVER

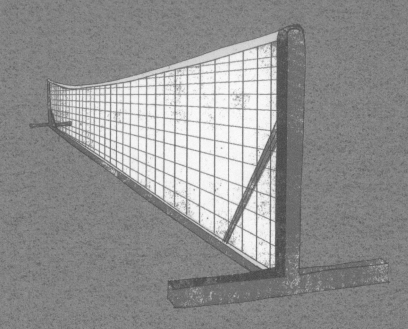

CHAPTER 1
BEFORE THE MATCH STARTS

PREPARING BEFORE a match is one of the most important ingredients to playing successfully.

The steps to prepare for a match are key to getting your mind organized on the process required for high-level focus in competition. Knowing you have done all the right things before you go to compete gives you a sense of confidence and improves your chances of playing well. From having your equipment organized properly to warming up your body for competition, here are some ways to position yourself for your best match performance possible.

1

Are You Equipped to Compete?

A critical part of mental preparation is to have the equipment you need ready to go before leaving for the competition. Knowing you are equipped with proper, reliable equipment is an important step to being mentally confident as you prepare for a match.

Advance preparation is one more item checked off on the to-do list for every level of player, from recreational to professional. Each item you check off will build your confidence as you prepare for your match. Confidence in your preparation can only help boost your confidence during the competition.

Important equipment preparation includes having two rackets of the same model, weight, and style with similar grips and overgrips. If you have to switch rackets in a match, it is important that the feel of each one be the same. Consider whether the rackets were strung at about the same time so that the string tension is similar if you have to switch rackets during a match due to a broken string, or just to change the match's mental momentum.

Are the grips prepared similarly? This affects the feel of the racket and ultimately how you compete; players are very kinesthetic in their approach to the game and are very aware of how their rackets feel. This is true not only for grips but also for the string, string tension, and balance point of the rackets.

Do you use an overgrip over the original grips? You want both rackets wrapped about the same so the feel is similar if you have to switch during a match. Change your overgrips often so they remain as absorbent and tacky as you like. Lastly, do you have spare overgrips in your bag in case of an emergency? Stopping to quickly change the overgrips in a match can also provide a mental pause to allow you to calm down or strategize a new game plan during a changeover.

The feel of the strings can change based upon the temperature during the match. Pros will often get their rackets restrung during a match as the temperature rises and falls; such fluctuations can greatly affect the tension of the strings and feel of the ball at contact. Of course, not everyone has access to that level of service. I make sure to adjust my string tension differently in the winter (looser) versus the summer (tighter), and I'm also careful not to leave my rackets in the trunk of my car—the heat or cold in there can affect string tension as well. This tension affects how contact with the ball feels and ultimately affects how you play during the match.

Make a checklist on your computer, phone, or notebook so you will know what you need to do to be completely prepared for a match. This checklist will also serve as a guide for your future preparations. It will become easier to add or subtract items as your experience as a competitive player evolves.

2

Look and Feel Ready to Play

Following the theme of "feel" for athletes, how your clothes fit and how you feel can greatly affect your mental preparation and approach to the match. Certain materials or colors, for example, may affect how you feel when you play. You may also have a lucky color you prefer based upon previous matches played.

There is a practical side to this as well. If you are competing in the summer and the conditions are hot or humid, you need to wear light-colored clothing that does not attract heat. You will also need additional shirts to change into if they collect too much sweat. This may help you feel fresh during a match, have a third set, or play back-to-back matches that day.

So much of the tennis game is dictated by movement and a player's ability to get into position to play their best shots. Your selection of shoes needs special attention for that reason. The type of shoe also needs to be suitable for the type of court surface you are competing on, for best traction and stability. Tennis shoes should provide strong lateral support, as 70 percent of your movement will be lateral. Proper fit is very important so that the comfort level of your shoes is not a distraction. Since everyone's foot is unique, you may have to experiment with different brands and models of shoes to find the best fit, comfort, and stability for your match performance. Remember that different court surfaces may require different traction features on the bottom of your shoes. This different traction feature is most evident if playing on clay courts or grass courts.

Socks are equally important to the feel and comfort of the feet. It is ideal to have extra socks to change into in case you have a third set or back-to-back matches. Several players wear thick socks called Thorlos. Other players wear two pairs of socks. One pair serves to pull moisture away from the foot or to add extra cushioning. Wearing two pairs—one thick near my foot and one thin on the outside—always gives me a quick drying effect and the most comfort.

Wristbands are also an important consideration on hot and humid days. They prevent sweat from rolling down into the palms of your hands as you play and allow you to wipe the sweat from your forehead or face when perspiring during competition.

Another important item to consider is a hand towel to dry your hands or face, shade yourself as you sit on crossovers between odd-numbered games, or dry off your grip between points. You may also use the towel to remove sunscreen you may have applied to your face or body from your hands. While the pros have large towels that the ball boys hand to them between points, most of us do not have that luxury. What you can do is keep a towel back behind you near the fence that you can personally access between points as needed to remove the sweat from your face, arms, or hands. It is important that any such activity fit into the 25 to 28 seconds between point time allowance to avoid a warning from an on-court official or the opponent questioning a delay of the game.

3

Don't Let Hunger or Thirst Be Your Opponent

||||||||||||||||||||||||||||||||||||||||||||||||||||||||||||||||||||||||||||||||||||||

Have your ever tried to compete when you were hungry? Not only is it a mental distraction, it can also zap your energy, which can have a negative effect on your focus when you need to compete at a high level. Energy bars are a great option for on-the-spot nutrition to avoid sugar lows or lack of energy during a long match. This nourishment can have a measurable effect on your ability to maintain your energy level and perform at your highest potential.

Proper hydration is also of utmost importance before a match. Most of our body is made up of water. As we compete and lose water from sweating, we need to replace it before it becomes a challenge that we don't need.

It is said that when you are thirsty, you are already 10 percent dehydrated. This by itself can affect how you perform, focus, and handle the pressure of competition. Hydration the night before as well as prior to and during the match is critical. Lack of proper hydration can cause cramping, loss of conditioning, and poor mental awareness during a match, which can lead to unnecessary match losses. In heavily humid or arid conditions, it becomes vitally important to have water or a sports drink that is not high in sugar or other unhealthy ingredients to stay hydrated during the game changeovers. I have seen many matches in the American South and desert regions where players had to be taken to the hospital for IVs.

4.

Stretch to Win

F lexibility is even more important than physical strength in tennis. Flexibility affects range of motion and the ability to quickly change directions and play with a natural looseness. In the past, athletes did static stretching while getting ready to play. However, research has shown that dynamic stretching is more appropriate for warming up the muscles and preparing them for a specific activity. There are proven advantages to stretches that engage the muscles in a variety of movements that replicate your performance in an upcoming competition. Dynamic stretching can include jumping jacks, side-to-side steps, use of elastic bands, and movements that resemble those you actually use in match play. Going through the swings you will use in competition and subsequent movement patterns can be a form of dynamic stretching as well.

You can identify appropriate dynamic stretches by searching for the term *dynamic stretching* online to find videos or books on dynamic stretches just for tennis. In addition, a personal trainer can design a program for your specific needs. Typically, you would perform this personal routine 10 to 15 minutes before going on the court. Between matches, you could do a modified number of exercises or decrease the length of time used for stretching. These exercises further prepare your mind and body for athletic performance.

Static stretches have been found to be more useful following competition. The idea is to stretch out or lengthen the muscles that have been contracted in the competition. Static stretching elongates the muscles and helps remove lactic acid from the muscles, which can reduce soreness in the hours and days following a match. Use of static stretching before competition is very old-school and is more relevant following competition.

5

Mood Music

Music has a strong effect on emotions. Certain music can put you in a relaxed, confident, or competitive frame of mind. Professional players use it all the time to block out the distraction of the outside world or to get psyched up before competition. What you choose to listen to, or the frame of mind you want to be in before competition, is very personal and can vary as your mood changes. It could be the theme from the *Rocky* movies, hard rock, or classical. Some players prefer to just be quiet; it's your choice.

Your mood music is very closely linked to something called neuro-linguistic programming, or NLP, which is embraced by author and life coach Anthony Robbins. Your memories of past successes or experiences can be linked to music, colors, environment, or sounds that you experienced during those emotional moments. You can revisit those positive experiences and actually feel as though you are experiencing them again by association with the anchor you relate to that experience.

A personal example is thinking of the color green. A very positive experience for me was playing in the PTR Nationals against the tournament number-one seed, Roy Barth. Roy had played at UCLA behind Arthur Ashe and was ranked as high as number 10 in the United States. That particular day I played exceptionally and defeated Roy in the first set. The courts that day were the green clay courts in Hilton Head. The windscreens were green, the tall pine trees were all green, and the overcast sky was a gray-greenish color. When I think of the color green, my mind goes back to that period. I can tell you how excited yet calm I felt, the crowd's response to our play, the cool breeze across my body, and how easily I moved across the court.

I use this and other anchored positive experiences to prepare for matches even today, more than 25 years later. I challenge you to think back to your own best performances, whether they were matches, sets, or games where you were performing at that unusually high level. You can again experience that feeling and use it to prepare for an upcoming competition. Add other similar experiences to your personal library to improve your mental preparation for your next match. Create your own personal "best of" memories—a mental mixtape, if you will—to remind yourself how well you have played in your best matches in the past.

Get in the mood to be your best champion.

"The ultimate tactic in the game of tennis is consistency. Consistency is your most devastating weapon."

—BILL TYM

ROGER FEDERER

is probably the most graceful of all players. His agility, balance, and coordination allow him to play with a seeming ease and grace that limit his injuries and fatigue in matches. His practice sessions are fun, and he plays creatively. Roger is an all-court player with many options in his game. He has continued to add weapons of mass confusion for his opponents as he has aged and grown his game. He tries shots and practices loose and smooth—like he plays. In his late 30s, he is still setting tennis records for wins and titles. He is perhaps one of the most loved players ever in the game of tennis. His most successful surface has been the grass courts like Wimbledon, and his most challenging surface has been the clay courts, where Nadal has dominated.

A Noteworthy Experience

I n school, you made notes of key items your teachers brought up in class. Those notes helped you study so you could perform well on tests. Notes were reminders of tips you felt were important to do well on your test. Now it's time to do the same for your next tennis match.

Similarly, most successful people journal their experiences for a variety of reasons. One is to help them recall or evaluate experiences. The process of recall, or visualization, will help you evaluate and determine what was important about the events you've experienced. Another reason to revisit your notes is to remind yourself of important or key moments for a similar upcoming event or activity. Reminding yourself of previous experiences allows you to recall how you adjusted to unexpected situations with positive results.

When I first started playing tennis as a freshman in college, I began keeping a journal of what I was learning and experiencing. I knew from experience that I would forget what I was learning or what I wanted to do the following day. Soon I had a history of what worked best for me as well as a history of all my match wins and losses and my responses to them. Taking time to record my emotional and strategic reactions allowed me to revisit them in a calmer mental state. Each revisit of those experiences allowed me to consider options to my match play responses and game-plan more successfully for the future. I now have notes from over 40 years of competition and a history to pass on to my son someday.

As a tennis player, you can incorporate these same practices into your game by keeping a journal or notebook with tennis tips that you keep in your bag. Reviewing your favorite tips will remind you of your game plan. Other tips will help you prepare for competition or make adjustments during the match as situations change. Pros on tour can actually be seen looking at their journals before a match. This allows them to think logically in the midst of the emotional battle being waged before a match and later, on the court. For example, I remind myself to stay positive during the match, follow my game plan, and take more time to reset my composure between points when I lose a point.

Reviewing your tips before a match is like a student reviewing their notes before taking a test in school. Looking at your tennis notes will help you pass the test of competition.

7

The Movies in Your Mind

We are a collection of pictures in our minds. Our experiences, past events, activities, and friends are stored in our minds for review. Visualization is perhaps one of the most important tools we have as players. When we prepare to do an activity, an event, or a competition, the image of how we did it before allows us to operate from a positive or negative mind-set. This movie in our mind creates a road map for our success going forward.

In preparation for a match, try to visualize in as much detail as possible the best you have played in the past. This is called *experience*. You will hear players refer to it often as a tool needed for knowing what to do in the present moment. Before a match, I find a quiet place with few distractions to picture or visualize how I want to approach the upcoming match. I see myself arriving at the site, collecting my equipment, checking in at the tournament desk, and going through my pre-match warm-ups.

My mental picture also would include me warming up with an opponent, first up close then moving back toward the baseline, taking our serves, and then doing our final equipment check before the start of the match.

The amount of detail in these visualized experiences will vary from player to player, based upon their personal preferred use of time. Visualization helps me feel comfortable going into the match, like I have been there before. It helps me feel confident.

Visualization can also remind me of past failures I plan to avoid. There are tendencies we all have to get down at certain points in matches or moments when our emotions get the best of us. These visualizations can help change your mental picture into how you would prefer to deal with those situations going forward. All the mental coaches use visualization to help their athletes recall past successes, forecast the future, and strengthen a player's self-confidence before competition.

You have the ability to choose a positive or negative move to direct your actions. Choose wisely.

8

Play It for Real

I n addition to visualizing, players may actually perform the physical movements they anticipate they
will use during their competition. Moving the body
through the motions you will use is an important part
of preparing for play. It is a rehearsal where you never
fail, and your body is experiencing what it will feel like
to make those movements later on during your match.

Using this type of training, you are combining
visualization with the physicality of performing certain
skills you will use in a match. I see pros practicing their
swings before going out on the court. This is letting the
nerves and muscles perform the skills that are expected
once the match starts. Physically rehearsing is much
like an actor or actress rehearsing their movements

before going onstage to perform. In other sports like baseball, the on-deck batter is physically rehearsing his swings before it's his turn to bat. He is also timing his swing to the actual motion the pitcher is making to the batter in the batter's box. This helps him adjust to the speed of the incoming ball and develop a sense of timing he will use once he is in the batter's box.

Professional tennis players rehearse their swings, quick movements, and changes of direction so that when they start to play, the muscles and the mind have already performed the skill, making it more automatic. The mind will usually remember the last movement you made. If that last movement was an error, you will see players rehearse the swing they intended to make to override the feeling of the error they just made. We call this move an "eraser." It erases the mistake and replaces it with what the player intended to do. While it is usually done physically, some players have the ability to do it in their mind, without the actual physical movement.

By actually performing the movements and swings before a game, without the interference of thinking about the ball, you will be better able to pay attention to the details of what you are performing.

Physical rehearsal allows you to feel how you will play tennis before the game.

9

What Time Is It?

You have organized well for the game. You have called the tournament desk or looked online to confirm your match time or are aware of adjustments to your start time. You know how long the travel time to the match site will be, and you are aware of heavy traffic times that might affect your travel. You know how early you need to arrive to allow time for hydrating, stretching, and mentally preparing before the start of your match.

Just like you would confirm your flight times before going to the airport, you should always confirm your match times. There may be rain delays, and matches can get backed up. Knowing you have the right time for your match is a huge mental confidence booster and stress reducer before match play.

Nothing causes anxiety like an unanticipated glitch before a match. You had it all planned out, with your routines all in order, only to experience an unexpected alteration. This can cause a jump in heart rate and a mental distraction from match play preparation. Just like adjustments during a match, you need to remain calm, look at the options, notify proper officials, and adjust your plan as best you can. Your ability to calmly adjust to the new challenges can allow you to have a positive approach to performing well. In fact, your adjustment to a situation may well give you confidence going into your match.

10

Your Road Map to Success

I know this sounds simple, but simple things are easily accomplished and build confidence. Simple things that have nothing to do with your athletic capability or physical skills can build confidence, but not paying attention to them can sabotage your success. For example, it's easy to get distracted and forget simple details in planning your trip to and from a match. Does your car have enough gas for the trip to the event and back home? Is there someone you need to pick up to ride with you?

What is the best path to your match play site? What is the best road map or app available for your location? Are you familiar with the directions to the site or local landmarks? All of these are important questions in deciding when you need to leave and will help reduce stress on the way to your match.

Depending upon the length of your trip, you may want to check for weather conditions or traffic that might affect your travel arrival time. All these are critical in reducing stress before you get to the actual competition. That will allow you to focus on your match preparation once you are at the site.

CHAPTER 2

A SMART START

THIS CHAPTER will introduce you to the key points in mental preparation and strategic decision-making to start your match wisely. You will learn to look for cues before the match as well as at the start of the match, to adjust your game plan as needed for that day and against that particular opponent.

This may include recognizing patterns, adjusting your game plan, and observing your own mental awareness levels during the match. I will go into more detail for each of the key components you may need to consider to be prepared to play your best tennis.

11

Sizing Up While Warming Up

As the match starts, be prepared to quickly analyze your opponent in the warm-up. You may pick up on clues as to your opponent's strengths and weaknesses on specific shots or preference of shots. You can also get information about your opponent by talking to their previous opponents. You may have actually watched your opponent play in an earlier match or had a friend scout their tendencies. This information is critical to deciding upon or adjusting your game plan against your particular opponent early in the match.

As much as you are assessing your opponent, it is important that you focus on warming up all of your own shots, with particular focus on moving your feet during the warm-up and getting your eyes trained to see the ball spin before you hit each shot. Your eyes staying focused on the ball is critical to judging when and where to move and when to execute your swing. Moving your head or your eyes before or during the swing will move your balance and affect your shot. This is commonly felt when you miss-hit a shot. While you're noticing your opponent's topspin, underspin, volleys, overheads, drop shots, and serves, remember it is more important to warm up all aspects of your own game so you will feel comfortable and in your zone as you start the match.

A word of caution, though: How an opponent warms up may not reflect how they actually play in the match. Some of this may be an intentional strategy on their part, or it may be completely unintentional. Some players are very lackluster in the warm-up, saving their energy for the start of the match. Their actual play is also influenced by the kind of ball you are giving them to hit against. I would suggest giving your opponent several speeds or heights to hit against to better determine what their capabilities really are. For the first few games in a set, I am usually very aware of what a player does in the actual match versus what they demonstrated in the warm-up.

The more I feel I know what to expect from my opponent, the better prepared I am to start my match successfully.

12

Find Their Dominant Side Early

A critical observation in the warm-up is noticing if your opponent is left- or right-handed. Too many matches are lost when players fail to do this. If your game plan is to play your shots to their backhand or their weaker side, you need to know which is their forehand or backhand. Most players commonly make the mistake of not observing this correctly until well into or even after the match. You also need to know which side your opponent prefers to hit from. This is easily discernable by hitting balls up the middle at the player and noticing which way they move to play their preferred side.

Notice your opponent's tendencies on certain shots. Do they back up when you hit deep balls and allow balls to fall into their strike zone? Their tendency to move back will allow you time to move forward and attack their return. If they choose to play a high loopy ball back in response to your shot, you may take a high return ball out of the air aggressively, which will allow you to take away their time to react to your shot.

Does your opponent move up and play your short balls on the rise or volley deep balls out of the air against you? Observe if they hit heavy topspin or demonstrate the ability to use underspin on certain kinds of balls you hit to them. This is important to anticipate returns and how you will attack or defend those types of shots. In fact, you may choose not to hit particular shots against them because you do not like to play against the kind of balls they return to you.

An important read is where they like to serve based upon the score in the game or set. Do they serve wide to the ad court on game points or up the middle of the service court to take your angled returns? If you are fast and like to run to balls, or if they have a very hard serve, do they serve at your body to reduce your ability to use your speed in returning or running down shots? Do they often jam you with hard and fast serves to cause weak returns they can attack?

Read your opponent to get a sense of their nervousness, their tendencies in situations, and how they respond to scoring pressure. Awareness of a player's body language is important to building your own confidence and sensing an opponent's vulnerability or their willingness to continue to compete. Be aware of your own body language to avoid giving cues to your opponent. This awareness will help you determine the effectiveness of your game plan and dominance in the match.

Similarly, look for signs of fatigue and frustration in your opponent. This means their racket might hang down between points, or they may be slouched over. You may notice them taking more time or appearing to be out of breath between points. They may begin to take more time on the changeovers in an attempt to regain their conditioning. Take advantage of these weaknesses by improving your level of commitment to staying focused as the points develop. I have seldom lost a match due to fatigue, so being in shape is a big mental advantage. Conditioning is a great weapon for outlasting an opponent. When conditioning fades, so does the willingness to compete and the ability to get into position and produce quality shots.

Developing a sense of how your opponent plays, their tendencies, and their patterns can be a positive deciding factor in your match. In effect, you are becoming your own coach.

13

Adjust Your Game Plan

As you begin to play your match using your carefully designed game plan, be aware that your opponent can adjust their game. This means you may need to adjust your game plan as well.

If you are winning, keep doing the same things that established your lead. If you are behind in the set, make adjustments to regain control of the momentum. This may include disrupting your opponent's style of play by changing your tactic. This usually involves eliminating early errors in the game, becoming steadier, and waiting for the right moment to hit more aggressively or go to the net, and especially staying positive with your self-comments and body language.

THE THREE MOMENTUM BREAKS IN A MATCH

There are usually three adjustment periods in a set. Going into play aware of this can help determine the outcome of the match. One such adjustment would be after the first three games: If a player is behind, they are likely to adjust their game style to change momentum in the match. Another one would be after the sixth game going into the seventh. The seventh game can take a set from 3-all to a 4-3 lead. The seventh game is usually described as a key moment in a match. The third momentum break is when a player has a lead of 4-1 or 5-2. At this point the player who's leading has a tendency to start entertaining thoughts of winning the set and may lose focus. The player who is behind realizes they are near losing and begins to play with more commitment than before.

The first three games of each set are critical to establishing control and momentum. If someone has a 3-0 lead, the player behind is going to adjust their game to get back into the set. So, if you are the one who is ahead, be prepared to withstand the new approach. You might see more lobs or safe play, or they may become more aggressive in their shot-making.

At 3-all or 4-2, the critical seventh game, a more strategic player will make a move to take the lead with a charge of energy or change of attack. This can come in the shape of more mental focus or a change of strategy in an attempt to throw the opponent temporarily out of control.

At 1-4 or 2-5, the player behind realizes they are about to lose and will make a final push to play without as much thought. They will choose a strategy to focus on and forget about all the reasons they are behind. The player in the lead will often think about the lead they have and hope the opponent gives up. They may also have thoughts about winning, getting ready for the next set, or trying to be too aggressive to close out the set. This momentum switch is common even at the pro level and is often talked about by the announcers in the booth.

An important tip to consider is: If you are winning, don't change a winning game. The pressure is on the opponent who is behind. If you are behind, you have nothing to lose. Pick out a game plan and play without fear of losing.

The opponent may try a variety of tactics like becoming aggressive and attempting to force you to return weak shots. They may also become more aggressive to avoid your pushing them back beyond the baseline and allowing you to attack their weak returns.

You need to be prepared for any balls that will come back to your side of the court quickly and aggressively. This awareness can enable you to neutralize their shots to stay in the point until you can take control of it. This adjustment may include an opportunity to angle your return shot and move the opponent off to one side of the court. Having moved the opponent off the court, you have created a larger target for your next shot and possibly forced them to make challenging shots on the run. Moving the opponent off the court may allow you to come to the net more often and end the point with a well-placed approach shot or volley.

14.

What Condition Is Your Focus In?

First, it is important to determine what is meant by *focus*. Coaches usually use this term to describe the degree to which a player is unaware of what is happening around them on other courts or who is watching. A high level of focus is being aware of what is happening at that moment only on your court and being prepared to take action on that situation. Imagine a scale of 1 to 10. If you can determine your focus level to be at 8 to 10, then you are highly focused and ready to perform at a high level. This is very important at the start of a match. With practice, you can use this scale as a reference, so when your opponent asks whether you are ready to start the match, you can assess where your focus is. When it's at a level of 8 to 10, you are ready to compete.

If you determine your focus level is at 5 to 7, you are not as likely to perform at your best, especially early in the match and at important points. To raise your level to 8 to 10, engage in active footwork in the warm-up to raise your intensity and energy level, as motion tends to create emotion, and focus on positive self-talk about how you love to compete and deal with challenges.

Should you determine your focus level to be below 5, you are probably going to perform poorly, with little focus and enthusiasm. Neither you nor your opponent will have a fun and challenging tennis experience.

This is an important awareness to use when you are warming up for the match, obviously. However, be aware if your focus level drops during your match. This can happen, especially when the score becomes critical, such as 4-1 or 5-2. This is where momentum often changes in a set. Does your focus level change when you play against a weaker opponent? Does it get higher against a higher skilled player? This is a reason most players lose to lower level players—because of their focus level. A practiced skill usually does not break down; the focus level drops, and that affects your shots the most.

Know what condition your focus is in!

"The game that takes place in the mind is played against such obstacles as lapses in concentration, nervousness, self-doubt, and self-condemnation. In short, it is played to overcome all habits of mind which inhibit excellence in performance."
— TIMOTHY GALLWEY

15

Move to Chase Away the Fear

As you start the match, know that it is important to stay energized when you compete. High-level players attempt to start a match with high energy and fast foot speed. They continue to move throughout a match to perform well.

Without a high level of movement, your positioning suffers. The lack of proper positioning will affect your ability to produce a quality shot. This may allow your opponent to get to balls that are not as deep and penetrating. Suddenly, they start to perform at a higher level, which can increase the fear of losing on your part. We all know it is only natural to become nervous as the value of each point and each game intensifies. The challenge is, how do you manage the fear? The nervousness can make your legs feel heavy, and your movement can slow.

Typically, a high-level player will average 8 to 10 steps between each ball they strike. This means they are moving in preparation even as their shot is going to the opponent's court and while they are awaiting its return. If someone asks me to evaluate a player's skill level, the first thing I look at is their movement to the ball and how they move once they have made their shot. Do they stop and wait for the opponent's shot, or are they moving to anticipate the opponent's return? Eliminating one or two steps between each shot can lower your emotional engagement in the point and produce a weaker position from which to hit quality shots. This lack of movement can only increase your fear of not playing well, which often causes continued loss of movement while you are trying to avoid a mistake and puts you in a poor position to produce a quality shot.

The best way to break the cycle of fear is to move! Run to go get a ball in the corner. Jump up and down—anything you can do to activate your feet to move quickly. You have to break the cycle of not moving as soon as possible. Watch the pros, and see how they move their feet quickly before the start of a point. They might jump up and down a few times to energize for the next point. See how they run out to the baseline following a changeover on odd-number games? Nadal will run out for the coin toss and move quickly even as the umpire is explaining the rules and making the toss. He is likely doing this in an attempt to break free from the shackles of fear. He is also using this as a motivational tool to start the match with high energy.

Use this strategy in fearful moments such as this; soon you'll be able to get back to playing your normal game at a level you expect to play—motion creates emotion.

JIMMY CONNORS

now retired, was the ultimate competitor. He never gave up. When he did lose, he said he merely ran out of time to solve the challenge of the match. His idea of practice was not bragging about how many hours he spent on the practice court but practicing as intensely as possible for a short period of time, just like players expected to perform in a real tennis match. Jimmy won 109 titles—more than anyone who has played the game. The only player close to him is Roger Federer, who passed 100 in 2019.

16

A Breath of Fresh Air

Breathing is critical to managing your nerves in competition. We have all experienced moments when panic set in and a friend would advise us to relax, just take a deep breath. Eventually we could feel our body and mind relax to a rational level. This advice applies to tennis anxiety as well.

When you become anxious in a match, your breathing is affected. You will have a tendency to breathe shallowly, which can increase the tension you feel in your body. When you feel that anxiety, you also may have a tendency to freeze up or not move for fear of making a mistake.

To avoid moments of panic or deal with them when they arise, first take a deep breath as you prepare to serve or receive a point. This will relax your body and get a good supply of oxygen in to prepare to play the point. Exhale as you contact the ball, just as you would when you lift weights. Exhaling at contact, as opposed to holding your breath, is extremely important to timing and relaxed effort in shot production.

Focus on breathing as you play to release tension and perform athletically. When you feel pressure in the match, you may have a tendency to hold your breath or breathe shallowly. This only intensifies the anxiety and tension in the body, and breathing is a great way to relax. You often see this happen when watching pro basketball players prepare to shoot free throws. They take a deep breath, relax their shoulders, and visualize the ball going through the basket before actually taking the shot. Before you begin to serve or receive, try to exhale deeply, then inhale deeply to get as much oxygen into your system as possible.

Play with a breath of fresh air to perform well in competition.

17

Rituals for Subconscious Performance

██

Rituals are important to improving your performance on a subconscious level. Players develop rituals that become habits and get them through challenging moments in matches in which thinking too much could make them play poorly. Proper rituals are important and usually develop over time based upon results from your own experiences or with a coach.

Rituals are particularly important for two critical shots in tennis: the serve and the return of serve. The preparation for serving in tennis is like preparing to shoot a free throw in basketball. When serving, pick out a target on the court, visualize the height you intend to aim to above the net, bounce the ball, breathe, and remove all thoughts. Now, look up to where you intend to toss the ball, see the shadow on the bottom of the ball or the spin on the ball to know you are actually seeing the ball, then keep your head and eyes at the point of contact as you strike the ball.

The serve is the first strike. But be prepared for the ball to come back. Analytics show that most points involve a serve plus one more ball.

Rituals to prepare to return the serve are important to put pressure on the opponent's serve. You need a ritual you always use to prepare for the best results. Your ritual will help you get to your opponent's serve and get it back in play or at least neutralize it. A mistake would be to return the serve, attempting a winner, particularly on a fast first serve. Instead, neutralize the offense of the server by getting the ball back into play and give yourself a chance. A good return of serve forces the server to be prepared to play another ball. If you are returning well, you apply pressure to the opponent to try to serve more aggressively. This can result in more missed first serves or double faults on their part.

A good routine would be to start farther back than where you intend to meet the ball. Activate your feet, move forward slightly as they toss the ball to serve, and adjust your feet to allow you to move into the return. You can also experiment with changing your receiving position in an attempt to distract the server from where they intend to serve or to improve your receiving position. Experiment against each opponent with where you need to be to improve your chances of getting the serve back in play and forcing them to make another shot.

Most returns involve a return of serve plus one more ball—be prepared to play the next ball back.

18

Manage Your Mind, Manage Your Game

I t's very natural to become nervous in anticipation of the outcome of your match. Both you and your opponent will have challenges managing the adrenaline rush of early-round match play. You want to be the one who exhibits calm and focus. That calmness in competition comes from relying on the rituals you have established in practice with your coach. Calmness is also a result of managing distracting thoughts and being centered in your mind.

One aspect of success in sports and in life is being able to manage your mind. When does your mind have a tendency to lose focus? Are there times in a match, times of the day, or kinds of opponents where you find yourself unable to manage your mind and therefore your performance? The better you prepare and game-plan, the less likely you are to fall prey to mismanaging your mind during competition.

Being able to answer these questions and your responses to them will help you understand how to manage the moments in your match in which you feel distracted and lose focus and momentum. Recognize when your mind tends to drift.

Loss of concentration is most likely to occur after a player wins the first three games of a set or once they have won the first set. In these instances, not only does a player's intensity drop, but their opponent's concentration most likely increases. It is essential that you identify these cues to help maintain your intensity and avoid losing momentum in a match.

In your postmatch review, I suggest that you document times in your match when you noticed this unwanted loss of focus. Work on a plan with a coach to ensure you can eliminate these slumps in future matches and further your growth as a mentally tough player.

19

Sometimes Better Lucky Than Good

Tennis pros are often heard saying, "There is a lot of skill involved in tennis, but luck is a factor as well."

Surprise winning shots, net-cord winners, and shanked returns by your opponent can cause you to feel unlucky and panicky. Know that your opponent will hit some of these shots, but so will you. Lucky shots have a tendency to equal out over the course of a match in most cases. Stay calm, accept them, and be prepared to play the next point with focus and confidence. This is another example of where ritualized responses to those types of shots are so important for staying in the moment and preparing for the next point.

You may be tempted to use an opponent's lucky shot as an excuse for why you are no longer winning. Some players do this, as it allows them to have something besides themselves to blame because they are losing. Resist the urge to be angry at your bad luck. This attitude can affect your motivation and distract you from competing in the moment. Eventually, with practice, you will perform at a level where you're not living in the past. You'll quickly forget your mistakes, except as reminders of corrections that you need to make going forward.

Rafa Nadal is probably the best example of letting go of any mistake or lucky shot by an opponent and immediately preparing for the next opportunity. He seems to always be in the moment.

20

A Swing and a Miss-Hit

There are days when the shots you usually count on are not working. Missing your "bread and butter" shots can have an adverse effect on your confidence. You may feel vulnerable without your normal weapons you rely on in competition. We have all seen top pros on days they were not able to play at the high level they're accustomed to. They will choose different weapons or tactics to survive that day or until they get back to their normal level of excellence.

Sometimes your opponent will not let you play your reliable shots because of the style of tennis they use against you. This is when you have to adapt an alternative style for that particular match or opponent. The more options you develop in your game, the more prepared you are for surviving when things don't go as planned.

When this happens—and it will—know that there are ways to combat this problem. Your options include selecting a larger target area for a while, staying focused on the ball longer, using positive self-talk, and looking for the spin on the ball as it comes to you to improve your reading of where it is coming and how fast, to help reduce unforced errors.

Set a goal of hitting more balls in a rally. This is a good way to put pressure on your opponent and find a way to work yourself back into the match. This strategy will give you more time to set up situations that allow you to be aggressive at appropriate times or just avoid losing points too quickly. Keeping the ball in play longer can apply more pressure on your opponent, as it increases the opportunity for them to make an error. You can change your style of play by experimenting to find a style that is working for you that particular day or is annoying to your opponent.

Often, I will go to the back fence, facing away from my opponent, and imagine that I am hanging all my negativity on the fence. Then, I take a deep breath, turn around to face the court, and begin with a refreshed attitude for the next point. In general, you want to reduce errors on usually reliable match play shots until your confidence returns.

The more you play, the more you will learn how important it is to trust your preparation, use positive self-talk, and hone your focus to stay in the moment.

Off days are not opportunities to permanently change your game, nor do they indicate you are not a good player. After such a match, go out on the practice courts, practice your dependable shots, and develop a depth of confidence in them again. They will usually come back to you quickly.

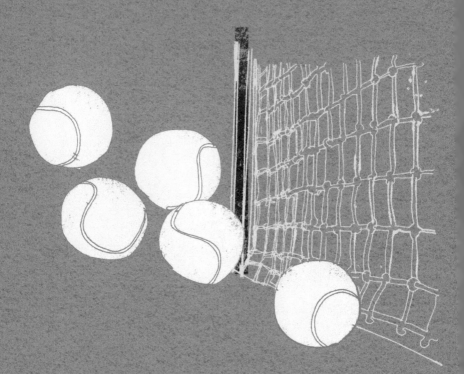

CHAPTER 3

A MENTAL MATCHUP

THE MENTAL part of tennis is the most critical part of match play performance. The mental game allows the physical game to be performed optimally. Most players perform better in practice than match play. That gap between practice and match play performance can be significantly reduced by preparation and understanding the successful tips of how to best play mentally.

21

The Mental Game in Singles

The game of tennis is perceived as a physical match between opponents. In reality, it is a mental chess match played in a physical environment. Much like a chess match, the players decide upon a plan of action to put an opponent in a vulnerable position and to capture the match. The mental skills actually drive the physical skills the players use.

Your ability to understand how an opponent thinks, what their patterns are, and how they respond to pressure will determine the physical skills you will use to defeat them.

As in most business, sports, or other situations in life, the more you know about your opponents, the better you can select an appropriate game plan as well as alternative plans of action throughout the course of the competition. The more you can learn ahead of time, the better you can plan your game going into the match. This will give you the confidence needed to play well as the match begins.

Every professional player you see has amazing physical skills and athleticism. The difference in the matches almost always comes down to who is better prepared mentally.

The mental game takes a little longer to develop than the physical game in tennis. The development is in the mind but greatly affects how the physical game is played. There are several books by former players and sports psychologists that can give you an introduction to how to think like a champion. All the concepts sound simple and fit into the category of recognition, but the practical application in the heat of the battle is challenging for even the best of players.

As a coach, I can watch a match between two highly ranked players objectively and diagnose their mental flaws. On the other hand, when I am on the court, I seem unable to recognize or correct the mental flaws in my own game.

Finding a coach is a very practical pathway to developing your mental skills with guidance. It does not even have to be a tennis coach, but someone who is known for their skills at helping any athlete understand the mental side of the game.

If you have been successful in business, in life, or in other sports, you can often apply your acquired knowledge to develop a strong mental tennis game.

"Relax physically between points. But never relax mentally until the match is over."
—BILL TILDEN

22

Playing Surfaces Can Be Rough

Your ability to analyze your physical environment can lead to a more confident approach to your match. For example, you should consider the surface you're playing on. Find out when the courts were last resurfaced, as this will provide an idea of how fast the ball will come off the court. A newly resurfaced court will have a slower and higher bounce after the ball strikes it. You may also discover that your traction on the court can be a little challenging on a new surface. New surfaces are rough, which can make it difficult to change directions quickly. There is also a chance of your shoe sticking and rolling your ankle on newly painted courts that have too much sand.

Older courts that have not been resurfaced in several years can cause the ball to bounce low and fast off the surface. You may be surprised by how fast a ball comes to you because of this type of surface. High school courts and some public park courts typically have not been resurfaced in two to five years or longer. These courts will play much faster. To adjust, you may have to use a shorter backswing, play further back to have more time to react to the ball, or move in and play more volleys so the ball does not contact the court.

Another factor to consider is whether the courts have windscreens, which most commercial and country clubs have. Windscreens provide a darker background and allow you to better see the ball off your opponent's racket. These screens also allow you to track the ball flight to your side of the court and assess the arc of the ball and speed of the incoming shot because of the contrast against the darker backdrop. Conversely, courts without windscreens make it challenging to pick up the toss of the server and depth of the ground strokes because of distractions you might see in the background.

Windscreens also assist in reducing the wind in the playing court, which can definitely affect the flight path of the ball. Hitting into the wind allows you to be a little more aggressive, as the wind will help keep your ball from going long. Hitting with the wind to your back will require more topspin to keep the ball from going long. You may have to adjust your shot landing point initially until you can get used to how much "carry" the wind is going to provide to your shots. There will be times when the wind is blowing across the courts from sideline to sideline. You will need to determine the direction and speed of the wind to know how much margin to allow, as the wind blows the ball into the court on one side or outside the doubles alley on the other side. Remember, when you switch sides, the wind will have the opposite effect on your shots. Make the mental adjustment on the changeover so you are not surprised. You don't want to make the adjustment after losing a point by not being aware.

Remember to make the necessary strategic adjustments as you change sides of the court on the odd-game changeovers. You may need to change your strategy so that it's the opposite of the previous game's.

23

Knowing the Score

Going into the match, you should be aware of the scoring for the tournament. Are the matches going to be full third sets of match tiebreakers in case each team wins one set? Depending upon the event or sanctioning rules, you may have to play a third set tiebreaker to determine who wins the match. Third set tiebreakers are called match tiebreakers. The match goes to the first player who wins 10 points and is ahead by at least two games over the opponent. The score, for example, would be 10-8, 10-7, or 10-6.

In the first or second set, if the score is 6-6, you would play a first set to 7 by 2-point tiebreaker to determine who wins the set. These are called set tiebreakers. You should practice playing both 7- and

10-point tiebreakers in your practice matches. Tiebreakers involve a different kind of strategy and mind-set from other set play. I would strongly suggest that you practice playing three out of five 10-point tiebreakers instead of two out of three sets to get used to the mental pressure of tiebreakers versus games. You will be amazed by how many matches go down to set and match play tiebreakers. Be prepared and you will have a distinct mental advantage. There will be an entire section explaining how to practice tiebreakers (page 128) to improve your game.

24

Know Your Strengths (Better Yet, Know Your Weaknesses)

||||||||||||||||||||||||||||||||||||||||||||||||||||||||||||||||||||||||||||

Constant physical and mental conditioning is an important factor in becoming a high-level singles player. You must also understand what your strengths and weaknesses are as a player and how others are going to attack your game. The more skills, tools, and weapons you can add to your game, the better you will be able to neutralize your weaknesses against a smart opponent.

It is important to play a variety of opponents so you are familiar with a variety of spins, tactics, and personalities. In your practices, try playing styles that you are not comfortable with at this point in time but would like to add to your game in the future. New skills require time before you can rely on them in competition. Adding underspin to your game is a great way to neutralize players with Western grips who do not like to come to the net. The lower-bouncing balls draw them up into the court and are challenging to play because of the position of the hand on the grip.

Develop other neutralizing shots that can buy you time when you are out of position or need to gain control of a point and position from any opponent who is pressuring you. A high loopy ball to the baseline with lots of spin can buy you time to recover, force a weak return from your opponent, or allow you to transition to an offensive position.

Keep developing weapons in your own game. Have a shot that you can attack the opponent with given the right time and position in the court. You need a shot that your opponent will recognize; when they see that you're about to play it, they will realize they are in a poor position to win the point because of the aggressiveness you exhibited previously. A strong or well-placed serve is a huge advantage to winning some free points. A consistent return of serve, one that always makes the server play another ball after their serve, is a great way to apply pressure on the serving team to try to hold serve. The ability to attack short balls that land around midcourt is critical to taking advantage of your opponent's weak returns.

Develop patterns that place you in favorable positions and your opponent in defensive situations. Recognize which patterns work well against particular styles of players, and have a variety of patterns to draw from if an opponent solves the initial challenge you presented. An example of a good pattern would be to place the ball high to your opponent's backhand until you receive a short ball in response, then attack to the forehand open court. Sometimes you may have to hit several balls to the opponent's backhand, then force them to move to the forehand to open up another opportunity to attack their weaker backhand again.

JOHN McENROE

During his playing career, John McEnroe was a fiery competitor with a short attention span. As a college player at Stanford, he did not like to practice or drill, so Coach Dick Gould made him play doubles. "Mac" loved to compete, and doubles helped him develop his serve and volley game, practice specialty shots like the lob, and underspin returns to a small part of the court away from the net man. Besides being a superb singles player, he became a world-class doubles player with Peter Fleming. When asked, "Who is the best doubles team in the world?" Peter would respond, "John McEnroe and whoever he is playing with." John was known for his left-handed serve and amazing volley skills in both singles and doubles. He was also known for his fiery temperament, which often upset opponents more than it affected his own game.

25

Analyzing Your Opponent's Singles Game

|||||||||||||||||||||||||||||||||||||||||||||||||||||||||||||||||||||||||||||||||

Knowing how to analyze an opponent's style of play is critical to playing with confidence. You can depend upon your coach, a friend, or previous experiences to determine your opponent's style of game prior to the match. This knowledge may allow you to practice and play against similar styles in your preparation for the match. At the very least, it may have provided you with information to devise a game plan that will give you confidence going into the match.

But if you're playing against an unknown opponent, there are ways to analyze their singles game. Their body type, for example, might provide an initial clue as to what to expect. A tall, strong-looking player might be a big server with powerful ground strokes. A smaller player in good physical condition might be a fast runner and consistent player. A heavier opponent might not be as fast but have powerful ground strokes. Body type is not necessarily an indicator of a player's style, but it might be a beginning point to anticipate the opponent's style of play.

Once the match starts, you can begin to read other cues as to their style of play, mobility, and shot selection skills. Mostly, be aware of opportunities to read a situation that might infuse you with confidence or a choice of game plan to use as the match develops.

26

Player Styles: The Strong, the Weak, and the Ugly

||||||||||||||||||||||||||||||||||||||||||||||||||||||||||||||||||||||||||

There are several categories in which to put an opponent's style of play. In addition to the ones listed, there can be many hybrid styles.

- Serve and volley player
- Aggressive baseliner
- Slicer-hacker
- Left-hander

I'll go into each style further in the next points. Once you have decided upon a general category your opponent fits into, you can begin to devise a game plan to use against them and determine which shots you will need to compete effectively against them. The better your game plan, the more likely it is that you will be prepared mentally through all three phases of the match: the start, the middle, and the closing. It is important that you have practice partners who simulate this variety of styles so you can gain experience in how to play against them in actual match play.

"I played and won some long matches in front of big crowds. It was my confidence that grew first, and that helped my strokes."
— BJÖRN BORG

27

Serve and Volley

|||||||||||||||||||||||||||||||||||||||||||||||||||||||||||||||||||||||||||||||||||

I f your opponent is a serve and volley player, they will be offensive and want to put pressure on you to make good returns or try to pass them as they come to the net. When playing against this style, you need to be able to get first serves back in play with some direction and depth. You can block the return of serve, underspin the return, or even lob the return, but it is important to give yourself a chance to get into the point and make the server play the next ball.

Trying to play aggressive returns against a strong first serve is usually not very effective, as its placement or ball speed is too fast for you to dictate how the point will be played. Taking speed off the serve by spinning the ball is usually more effective. Use an underspin or topspin ball to dip the ball in front of the charging player. This tactic is called neutralizing, or taking away the advantage the server has with their serve, just to get the ball back in play or back to even out the point. Usually cross court is a safer return against this player and limits their options in returning the ball back toward you. If you return down the line, they have an angle return against you. You would want a shorter backswing, as you will have little time to execute a full swing against a fast serve. Use the speed of their serve to your advantage by redirecting the serve with placement.

This player's second serve will typically be a little slower and with more spin to get it in play. On their second serve, you can be a little more offensive. You might move forward into the court as you make a more aggressive return or take away their time to get to the net behind their serve. If the serve falls into your strike zone, you may even choose to become more aggressive with your return while still using a lot of spin. The more spin you hit, the more challenging it becomes for the player attempting to volley to control the spin of the ball off their racket for accuracy.

Another good tip is to change your receiving position and try to force them to serve into your strength.

Because the second serve is a little slower than the first and will likely bounce a little higher, it becomes easier to lob the return versus trying to lob a first serve. The lob return is a great shot to practice against an opponent who does not typically have a hard serve. This will help you when you are facing a server of higher level in a match situation.

While the lob return might be a little challenging to execute consistently, it certainly is an option to keep the server away from the net. You might move to your left or right to expose a particular opening for the server in an attempt to make them serve where you want them to serve. This could put pressure on them to try to serve into a smaller target, or to serve into a strength you have teased them into serving into.

Here is a list of things not to do: Don't stay back and try to smash hard returns; avoid using hard slices, as they have a tendency to float; and don't miss. Make the volleyer have to play the ball off your return—no free points for them!

The strategy of a serve and volley player is to keep the receiver off balance with surprise, speed, or direction of the serve. If your serve is strong, a good return would be serving at the player's body. This serve will limit options of intentionally angled returns and keep the receiver's hands near their body, thus limiting control of the direction and speed of the return. A wide serve out toward the alley can pull the player off the court and open up large areas to close in on the net and volley to the open space created by the wide serve. A serve up the center or the "T" can reduce the angles a returner has to pass a serve and volley player.

As a server, you have three optimal directions: wide to the alley, into the receiver's body, or up the center. Mixing these three directions can keep your opponent off balance just enough to make their return of serve a little less controllable as far as direction and speed. Mixing those three directions with a variety of spins will keep the receiver guessing as to what to expect from your serve.

28

Aggressive Baseliner

The aggressive baseliner will typically have a strong forehand, and you will have to find a way to neutralize that weapon. A good strategy is to hit wide to their forehand to pull them wide to that side. This will open up the court to their backhand side, which they will have to hit on the run. Big forehanders like to hang out in the backhand court and rip forehands. Once you get them off to their backhand side, you can take them wide to their strong side, and then you will have exposed their backhand side as a big target they have to cover on the run.

Aggressive big hitters like the ball about waist height or higher. Against this player, an underspin shot to keep the ball low—at or below net level—is a good play. This makes it challenging for them to rip big shots as aggressively. Roger Federer is famous for this shot: He hits an underspin backhand low and short to the opponent's backhand to force them to move up into the court and hit up to him. In this way, he dictates the next ball deep to them and hits behind them or into the open court. You will want to change the speed of your shots to avoid giving the big hitters a rhythm to hit against. Try serving and volleying to their backhand to take away their big forehand on your serve game. Often, they will gamble and try to run around the serve to the backhand in an attempt to hit a forehand. In this case, a serve up the middle of the court will result in an ace for you.

The biggest factor in playing an aggressive baseliner is to avoid getting discouraged if they hit a lot of winners. Trust me, they will also make a lot of errors. Get a lot of balls back, let them try to keep slugging winners, and don't try to outhit them at their own game. You could also come to the net against their backhand and apply pressure to pass off their weaker side. When serving, serve into their body to force them to move away from the return instead of moving into the return and using their power.

ARTHUR ASHE

grew up in the southern United States, attended UCLA, and played for the US Army. Arthur was a strong serve and volley player. He experienced the world of racism as a player. But his sense of purpose and right and wrong allowed him to be a leader in equality. His relationship with Nelson Mandela allowed Arthur to influence the world in this area. When Arthur reached the finals at Wimbledon and faced Jimmy Connors, who had beaten him several times, Arthur and his coach devised a plan to take Jimmy out of his game. Jimmy loved to play against power and was better at that game than Arthur. So, Arthur took most of the pace out of his game that day. He used underspin to create lower-bouncing shots and softer-hit balls to destroy the rhythm that Jimmy liked to hit against. As a result, Arthur became a Wimbledon champion.

29

The Slicer-Hacker

Playing the slicer-hacker opponent is very challenging. They provide you with nothing with which to beat them. They keep you off balance and guessing as to what kind of ball you will receive or even how it will bounce to you. You will need very good closing skills to beat this opponent.

Your strategy here is to get to the net and volley as many shots as possible. Once their ball bounces, it is very unpredictable. When they hit the unpredictable underspin and sidespin shots, you will have to stay low to the court and probably use underspin against their shots as well, because of the unpredictability of how their ball will bounce. Unfortunately, this match will not be the prettiest. Like the famous tennis pro Brad

Gilbert said, you'll have to "play ugly tennis" (a style that is difficult for an opponent to play against) to win, or at least to keep them from winning. Brad was able to beat players who were considered better than him by playing ugly shots in the match.

Another "ugly" tactic is to play high loopy shots from the baseline to neutralize your slicer-hacker opponent's underspin shots. The height of the ball above their shoulder makes it more challenging for them to control how they will play the ball back to you. You can also bring them to the net with your drop shots to limit their ugly shots to you. This tactic would then allow you to lob them or attempt a passing shot. You might also try to serve and volley against them, but you have to move your feet a lot to volley because their slice and hack shots curve a lot in the air and react unusually off your racket. You will need lots of footwork to get into position and really focus on the ball to be ready to cut off their spin return before it can bounce and cause you difficulty.

You should not try to rip your ground strokes that are well below the net against this type of player. When you do close in to volley, be aware: Slicer-hackers usually like to lob a net player. The key here is lots of small adjusting steps, seeing the ball well, and having a safe target for your shots.

30

Left-handers

The next challenge is the left-handed player. Because there are fewer left-handed players in the game, their shots are unusual; you have to remember that a shot to a right-hander's backhand is actually a ball to the lefty's forehand. The real challenge comes in returning their serves. The spin on their serve will curve in the opposite direction of a right-handed server's spin. Lefties are famous for serving wide to a right-hander's backhand side and pulling them wide off the court on the ad court side. In the deuce court they can curve the ball away from the right-hander's backhand up the middle, or the curve of the server will move into the right-hander's body and jam them when trying to return the serve.

One of your best options in playing a left-handed opponent is to move farther to your left, so they cannot pull you so wide off the court on the ad court side. You could also move forward to attempt to cut off the angle of the lefty's wide serve. Using underspin when you are pulled wide will give you a better chance of getting the return in play than attempting topspin with the ball moving away from you. The underspin can allow you to get more on the outside of the ball and pull it back into the court across your body. Because of the curve of the lefty spin, it is usually best to try to return cross court instead of down the line. This is especially true in the deuce court when they serve wide to your forehand. Their spin can make the return curve uncharacteristically wide if you attempt to return down the line. As a last option, try to lob more on the returns to at least get the ball in play. Better yet, schedule lots of practice matches against left-handed players to get more accustomed to the options they have and how you will respond to those options.

One of the things you do not want to do when playing a left-handed opponent is hit hard returns and miss too often—that just equals free points for them. Above all, don't let them see you get discouraged. As a director of tennis, I was always fortunate to have lefty tennis pros on my staff to hit against. Practice time against them made it a little easier to face a lefty player in my next tournament.

"Don't just watch your opponent's strokes; watch his attitudes and habits."
—HARRY HOPMAN

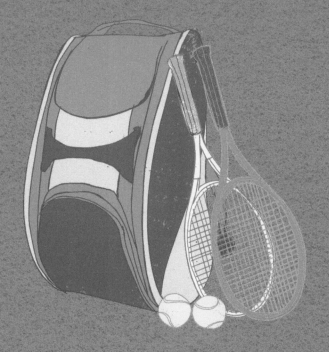

CHAPTER 4

DOUBLE YOUR CHANCE
OF SUCCESS

DOUBLES IS the game most often played by recreational and club players in USTA leagues. As players age, they often prefer not to run as much as singles requires. Doubles players often prefer the team connection and having a partner to share the pressure of the match and strategize with during the competition. Having a partner can give you an emotional outlet in times of frustration.

As a doubles player, you're required to use more volleys, overheads, and approach shots than most singles players. Singles players like John McEnroe improved his singles skills with the variety of shots used in doubles. There are traditional formations that are suggested starting points for doubles players, but once you have a little experience, there are many options as far as the positions a team can use to influence a doubles match.

In this section, we will look at not only the game of doubles but how to play a variety of styles and the mental skills required for doubles as a team sport.

31

Traditional Doubles Formations

A doubles player must know the job description
for four different positions on the court: server,
server's partner, receiver, and receiver's partner. Each
position has special skill sets and suggested strategical
and tactical options, and they all require practice.

Servers typically serve from a position on the
baseline that is halfway between the doubles alley and
the center of the court. The priority is to attempt to
get the first serve in play to the receiver's service box
and to the side, forehand, or backhand that will cause
them the most difficulty to return consistently. It is
important to have a plan before serving and tell your
partner where you are attempting to direct the serve.
This will allow them to have a better idea of how the

return will come back and be prepared to intercept the return as a poach.

A server's partner, the net player, is about halfway between the net and service line in the ad court service box to start the point. The server's partner should be prepared to distract (legally) the receiver and attempt to intercept the receiver's return of the serve and volley the ball for a winning point. The server should communicate to the net player where they are attempting to direct the serve to allow the net player to be prepared to intercept the return of serve.

The receiver of the serve will stand behind the baseline on the right, or deuce court, and attempt to return the serve cross court to the server's side of the doubles court and away from the server's partner at the net. Have a plan as to where you want to make the return of serve, even to the point of telling your partner where you plan to attempt to return the serve. This will help you play with better purpose when returning. The return can be cross court, a lob over the server's partner, or an attempted down-the-line return toward the net player's alley.

The receiver's partner is on the left or ad court service line, usually to start the point. Their job is to determine if the serve lands in the correct service box for their partner. Once the serve is in, and the receiver has returned the ball past the server's net player, this player will attempt to move forward and distract or intercept the return by the other team. This person is often the key player in a point, once they know how to move correctly and at the right time.

These are suggested starting positions and simple job descriptions for each position. I suggest watching live or televised doubles games to see the basics of how the game is played and how the players move in each of their positions in a match. You and your partner can choose from multiple options to better take advantage of your particular skill set or to distract the serving or receiving team, which we will discuss later in the book.

32

Preparing for Atypical Styles of Play

While most teams play a conventional doubles style, atypical styles can prove very distracting. Team awareness and communication become very important to recognize unusual styles and outline a game plan against them. When someone creates an atypical formation, immediately call a time-out to talk to your partner about what your team wants to do to combat the formation. At least stop to be sure you have a plan, and do not freak out because of the formation.

I suggest you try an atypical doubles position in your practice matches to avoid becoming distracted when you see it used against you in match play. You should practice using atypical positions yourself to determine if you could use them against opponents in your matches to change the momentum to your advantage. Knowing how to play these formations opens up all kinds of options in a match to combat a tough opponent, change the momentum, or neutralize a particularly challenging team.

"Every time you win, it diminishes the fear a little bit. You never really cancel the fear of losing; you keep challenging it."

—ARTHUR ASHE

33

Strengths and Weaknesses of Atypical Styles in Doubles

Players rely on these unusual styles to show you a game approach you are unprepared to compete against. They usually take pride in being unusual, knowing they create havoc with their approach to the game. These players know their own weaknesses and have devised a game plan or formation to hide that weakness to a high degree. At the same time, does their atypical style end up providing opportunities for them to capitalize on their strengths?

You and your doubles partner need to quickly determine the other team's strengths and how you plan to counter them with your own team's strengths or neutralize them with counter moves. This could be serving at their body to eliminate angles, lobbing to take away aggressive net play, or both you and your partner moving back to the baseline and lobbing returns to neutralize their aggressive style. The answer is to develop the skills necessary to analyze these situations, tactically counter them, and build on your experiences so you can devise a positive plan of action.

It is up to my partner and me to figure out what our opponent's atypical style happens to be and how best to counter it. Our communication skills as a team are on display in this situation. We need to communicate what our options are based upon our skill set and what their strengths are and determine how best to attack their team.

We look at grips that might limit their shot-making skills or how they handle underspin or high-bouncing topspin and whether they are agile around the court or slow afoot. One partner can often compensate for another partner's weakness and perhaps nullify that weakness in the match. Do they crowd the net aggressively frequently, indicating their weakness is an inability to cover a lob? Does their fear of the net expose them to drop shots and short chip shots, forcing them to move forward on your terms?

An example of an atypical doubles style is one in which both players play back. They take away the advantage of poaching and set themselves up to be a consistent lobbing team. This team often has weak serving partners and weak volley games. They seldom lose points by errors but can cause you to make lots of errors if you overhit shots in an attempt to win points easily.

Another atypical style is one up and one back. These teams usually have one player that does not like the net but can keep the ball in play until their partner at the net can cut off shots by the opponents. Against this team you can attempt to bring the baseliner to the net with drop shots or short chip shots. You can also lob over the net player and try to come to the net to take away their formation. Teams that serve and volley are another challenge, because they attack the net and take away your areas in which to aim the ball or react to their quick volley returns. Better have a lob in your game to get them off the net when they come in to volley.

Be mindful when there are two lefties on one team. This team changes the kind of spin you receive, changes your return targets, and requires conscious awareness of what to expect from their spin and how to play opposite targets. Their serves can be challenging for several games until you can begin to understand how their spin affects your shots. By then you may be behind a few games. Schedule some practice matches with lefties to give yourself a chance to win.

You got this.

"Everyone needs a coach, friend, or family member who can see what they are doing when you cannot see it."

—PETE SAMPRAS

34.

Psyching out Opponents

P syching out your opponent is a tactic that can be mental or physical. It causes your opponents to become distracted, feel uneasy, and prefer not to play against you or feel intimidated to the point where it affects their level of tennis performance.

Tactics like this could include delaying the speed of the game, making questionable line calls, intentionally aiming for an opponent with your shots, or a variety of other tactics that make the other team feel angry or insecure. When the momentum of a match is with the opponents and the game feels like it is going by too fast, you can slow the momentum by talking to your partner, pausing to catch your breath, and attempting to reset your mind about what can be done to regain control of the match.

In most cases, questionable line calls are not made intentionally. Each player has a different view of the ball's position and whether it lands near the line. If you experience such a call, it is within your rights to question it. Most calls are made because the player making the call anticipated where the ball would land or had a bad angle to make the call. Ultimately, the team who made the call has the final say. If questionable calls continue, you may call an official to your court to assist. You can ask the official if they saw the ball in or out following the call that was made. You can see on television how often players questions calls, and most of the time they are wrong.

There may be times when you feel your opponent is hitting at you. Most likely the ball hit at you was not intentional. Often you were just in the line of fire for their shot. This does usually provoke anger or an adrenaline rush that you will have to manage during the match. I suggest you do not take it personally; just continue to play the game. In the 2019 Wimbledon doubles finals, one player was hit three times by the opponents. He got up each time, and the match continued. Mentally tough for sure.

To handle this attempted distraction, whether intentional or unintentional, you must be very self-confident, have strong team chemistry, and be confident in your knowledge of the rules. This includes knowing when to ask for help from an on-site tournament official.

"Learn a lesson every time you lose."
—JOHN McENROE

35

Psyching Yourself Out

Often it is not your opponent psyching you out: It is you. It is natural to become worried about whether your equipment will hold up for the match or whether you have enough stamina to make it through a match. Even the reputation of your opponent can be intimidating.

As you already know, preparing your equipment well before going to competition can alleviate worries during a match. You also have learned that proper training, nutrition, and hydration before and during a match can alleviate the fear of not having the stamina to finish. In other words, preparation can help avoid those distracting thoughts.

Now, let's discuss how to avoid letting yourself get psyched out by an opponent's reputation. Worrying about a player's seeding or reputation, or their being a better player than you, is a way to psych yourself out for sure. Perhaps the best way to manage the fear of the ranked opponent is to focus on your own game plan. Look at the match as a great opportunity to see how you match up against a higher-ranked player. You have nothing to lose—they do. In doubles, talk to your partner to stay focused, and enjoy the opportunity to play against such a high-level opponent.

In doubles, coming together to game-plan during the match and talking about where you plan to serve or return serve can help you stay in the moment. My partner and I used to have a contest to see who made the fewest mistakes in the net during each set as a goal to keep us focused. Sometimes we would decide if we were able to win three games in each set, we would consider ourselves winners.

SERENA WILLIAMS

Serena Williams grew up in Compton, California, and was coached by her father. Serena is an all-court player with dominating power and willpower. She has won over 20 grand-slam titles and trails only Margaret Court in total titles won. Her sister, Venus, was the star initially. Tall and agile, Venus got most of the attention as the sisters grew into prominence in the world of tennis. But their father, Richard, said Serena would be the champion. Her intensity, strength, and athleticism on and off the court would soon prove her father correct. Serena has dominated women's tennis and made everyone become more physical just to be able to compete against her. Serena is the most feared player to face in a tournament draw. Smart on and off the court, both she and Venus have proven to be successful businesswomen as well.

36

Selecting a Partner

In doubles, you and your partner need to be compatible. The chemistry of your team can be a determining factor in success, as in any team sport. You need to communicate with one another, keep each other positive in challenging moments, and agree on strategies and tactics before and during a match. All of this gives you the best chance to pull out a victory.

Styles of play are very important in matching partners. Two aggressive, big-hitting players are usually not a winning combination. Every strong team needs a sitter and a hitter. That means one of you needs to be a player who is steady and can set points up and keep the ball in play, and one of you needs to be the more aggressive player to put the ball away.

Having a left- and right-handed combination on a team can prove very successful. Some teams prefer to keep the forehands to the outside of the court. For example, that would mean your right-handed player is in the deuce court and your left-handed player is in the ad court. Lower-level players often hit the ball late so it goes down the line or they worry about the net player—so the ball goes to the net player. At the higher level of play, some teams prefer to keep the forehands to the inside, as that is where most high-level players keep the ball directed, down the middle. Top-level players challenge you to go down the line because it is a higher risk shot.

Two steady players can cause a lot of problems for other teams that cannot keep the ball in play. The aggressive team will rely upon trying to hit winners and most often will make too many errors. Steady players can frustrate teams because they change the ball to a slower speed and neutralize the opponent's power, and as a result can often upset higher-level teams.

Communication also plays into a team's success. As part of a winning team, it is important for you and your partner to talk between each point that is played. Your discussion usually involves a reset in attention to what is happening; determining strategy for the next point, places to serve, poach, and return serve; or adjusting your team's position to affect strategy. Even when your team decides on a serving or receiving plan, you can use hand signals to reaffirm the decision before the point starts. While it is a reaffirmation for the team, this kind of continual communication also reminds the opposing team that you have a plan.

Communication style is also important for a team. Do you and your partner both like to talk and strategize between points, or is one of you the type who does not like to talk between points, as they find it distracting? Having a partner who enjoys talking a lot between points can be annoying if you prefer to not talk much or at all. It is important to have a partner who matches your style of dealing with the time between points. Statistics show that in a 90-minute match, there are only 12 to 15 minutes of actual play time. That means you have an hour and 15 minutes of time between points to communicate with your partner.

Learn your partner's communication preferences for match play. Also, discuss how you both prefer to break down what happened following a match, so you can improve as a team for future competitions.

Choose partners wisely, and be willing to adjust your own communication style, if necessary.

37

The Mental Game in Doubles

With four players on the court, the mental game becomes more complicated. You have to feel comfortable with your partner. However, the dynamics of the other team's personalities has an effect on you and your partner as well. Personalities can be intimidating or even annoying to the point where they become distracting for a player or a team. Even body language and style of play can be distracting for you or your partner. This is when you and your partner need to keep each other focused on the match and your strategy instead of on your opponents.

One positive aspect of doubles is teamwork. You can be having a challenging day on the court, and your partner will hold you up until you get your game together. Conversely, your partner can have an off day, and your energy and positive talk can support them until they get back into the game. In the heat of competition, it can be difficult to analyze what you are really doing. Having a partner can provide you with an objective point of view, which will help you in assessing a given situation and choosing appropriate responses. For example, you might ask each other: Should we stay back on the first serve and move up on the second serve, should we attempt to lob the net player, or should we hit at the net player to try to intimidate them?

Tennis is a challenging game because of the unique scoring system. You are never so far ahead in a match that you are not at risk of losing or so far behind that you cannot come back to pull out a victory. Momentum can change quickly because of the scoring within the game or set. At the end of a set, your wins do not carry forward with you. You may have won the set 6-0, but you start all over again for the second set. This is unlike baseball and football, where you build on your score after each inning or quarter.

38

Developing a Team Game Plan: Who Serves First?

Going into a tennis match, a team should create a game plan, starting with decisions about the first serve. If you win the spin, do you choose to serve first or receive first? You should also know who will serve first for your team. For this decision, consider time of day, where the sun will be, who handles serving in the sun best, and what server and net player combination is the strongest to best win the first service game.

In morning matches, I prefer to serve first. I am a morning person and usually well prepared to start. Often my opponents are not as focused, and I always feel I can get a few free points early in the set.

Depending upon the sun, I may choose to make the opponent serve first on the sunny side in hopes of breaking their serve. I have never minded serving in the sun because I have a good variety of serve positions from which to toss the ball so as not to affect the speed or location of my serve games.

If you are serving first, do you want to jam or serve into the body of the receiving team to limit angled returns? If receiving first, do you want to lob the first couple of points to keep the net player from poaching on the return, or do you prefer to chip the return and charge the net?

I have always preferred to lob early in the game on second serves. That has a tendency to make the net player hesitant to poach too early. They often back off the net slightly in anticipation of a lob, which opens up the return lanes for my cross-court returns.

Once you and your partner have decided on a beginning strategy, you will continually adjust the team game plan as the match unfolds, based upon score or tactical needs.

39

Analyzing Doubles Teams to Gain an Advantage

E arly in the warm-up, determine how your opponents like to play—aggressive, or steady with few errors? Recognizing the other team's style of play can help your team determine how to establish your game plan during the start of the match. There will be another moment toward the middle of the set when teams adjust to how the match is being played, usually initiated by the team that is behind. There will normally be a strategy change as the set is about to be completed as well, typically instigated by the team that is behind in an attempt to avoid losing the set.

If a player makes too many errors, you can see their partner often becomes a little anxious about trusting that person to make good decisions. Therefore, you get some dissension between players.

Practicing against a variety of teams with different styles can help you recognize a style in a match and have a reference point with which to plan your attack. Most opponents do not play like the regular foursome you play at the club every week. Try to get your group to implement different styles of play, bring in a new player, or make everyone play an unusual style of play each week. This will better enable you to assess different types of play, have experience playing against those styles, and understand how to compete against them.

Be aware of these three stages in each set to maintain control of the match.

As the match develops, notice whether the opposition communicates with each other. Notice their reaction to the three stages mentioned earlier in each set: the first three games, the seventh game, and the closing out of the sets. Are they acting as a team, or are they just two players playing singles on a doubles court? Look for particular aggressiveness in their strokes or net play. Be aware of how different teams respond to pressure to better understand the options you can use against them. Do you have any knowledge of their previous play patterns? Any insight into their game can provide confidence in your game planning. Having practiced against a variety of styles, you can say, "They play just like the team we practiced against last." As a result, you have the experience to know how best to handle their style of play. A key distinguishable point is to notice if one player is left-handed, which would affect your game planning.

40

Tips on Analyzing
a Team's Style

W hat should you look for early in the warm-up?
Does the player practicing volleys have a
technique that looks like they can direct the ball well?
If not, aim a lot of short balls in your court at the net
player. Do their warm-up overheads look reliable? If
they're not very solid, this will tell you if you should
lob the opponents anytime they come to the net.

Do the serves look like they are attackable because
of a lack of speed or depth? Do you need to stand
farther back because the first serve is very fast, and
you need more time to read how you want to return
it? Perhaps there is a big difference in the speed of

the first serve versus the second serve. Be prepared to attack the second serve. Notice if the opponent seems hesitant to move up to short shots or they hit them but retreat to the baseline.

Are the opponents a team that stays back and lobs or serves and rushes the net? Or perhaps one player attempts to control the net on every point while their partner runs down all the lobs. Develop a checklist of items to evaluate teams that you will play against. This list can include the tips discussed here or your own tips you begin to recognize from your match play. This checklist, and your continued experience, will provide you with a strategy to use against a team as well as to help you anticipate how they will compete against your team.

STEFFI GRAF

Originally from Germany, Steffi Graf is an incredibly athletic and focused player. Coached by her father during her career, she possessed a huge forehand and a devastating underspin backhand. The opposite dynamics of her spin forehand and backhand along with her speed made her one of the top women players of all time. Nicknamed "Fraulein Forehand" by Bud Collins, Steffi would capture more than 20 Grand Slam titles. Steffi was swift afoot and in great physical condition. On a side note, Steffi and Andre Agassi married in 2001. Collectively, they have earned more Grand Slam titles than any other married couple.

41

Strengths and Weaknesses of Typical Doubles Teams

There are a couple of simple things to look for in analyzing an opposing team. Once you recognize the tendencies of a team, it becomes easier to determine their strengths and how you might anticipate their play.

Identifying a player who has a strong and consistent first serve, for example, will determine how effectively you can game-plan to return serve. This type of server can set up their net player to be aggressive against your returns. You may ask your partner to join you on the baseline when you are returning serve, until you feel comfortable getting the serve back in play and away from the server's net player. A weaker server could provide you an opportunity to make stronger returns and attack the opponents by going to the net more often in the match on your return of service games.

Doubles teams may not have equally skilled players. When you determine a player is weaker, you have a point of attack to break down the team by directing more balls to that player. Determine if both players prefer to come to the net to play points. If so, you will want to lob them more often to keep that team from becoming too aggressive. You may also use the option to hit passing shots between the players and force them to decide who should play the ball. This tactic will also reduce your tendency to hit shots wide under pressure.

If a team likes to play one player at the net and one player on the baseline, it becomes easier to anticipate when and where to lob over the player who is nearest the net. Because most teams do not serve and volley, you might hit drop shots or short balls to the player who stays back on the baseline, forcing them to move forward into an uncomfortable position near the net. Once they come forward, you can aim between them, take advantage of their lack of net skills, or simply lob over them into the backcourt.

While the typical doubles position may look one way at the start of the game, always be aware that teams may adjust their style during the game. You need to realize what alignment changes they are using once the ball is in play. This could be one of your own tactics. In fact, your team may show a typical alignment on purpose, then switch to an unusual formation once the point is in play.

42

Using Unusual Doubles Formations

This is my favorite tactic to use in matches. I like being creative, and unusual formations keep my attention at a high level. I feel most teams do not face these formations often, and using them gives my partner and me a huge advantage of surprise and disguise that can change a match at any moment.

Because there are few rules concerning how or where players start or move to in a match, there are many formation options that opponents may not have seen before. Unusual doubles formations are great momentum changers to use at a challenging moment in a match. They can catch your opposing team by surprise and force an error due to their uncertainty about what option to choose against your formation.

Sometimes we will serve with the server's partner standing behind the server. When the serve is hit, both players will move in a previously discussed position. We often return serve with me standing behind my partner, who is receiving serve. If the serve goes toward the alley from behind, I will break to the left. If the serve is up the middle in the deuce court, my partner will return serve and move toward the open court, and I will move up to their former return position.

I was able to win a PTR National Championship Mixed Doubles by playing some very unusual formations throughout the match, which totally confused our opponents. It is important to get your partner's approval, and you should practice the formations before using them in a match situation.

One example of an unusual doubles formation is both players on the baseline while the partner is serving or while they are receiving. This takes away the net person as a target and means the team on the baseline has to be concerned only with moving forward. If you're the serving team, you might play one of many I-formations to force an opponent to change the direction of the return of serve or just distract the receiver.

The weaker team might use unusual formations of any kind to psych out the opponent. This strategy can be a great neutralizing opportunity to change the momentum in a game or set. If you find that you're the weaker team, this can take away the advantage of a stronger team.

These unusual doubles formation options should be well practiced before attempting to use them in a match situation. You should be familiar with how they affect your own team as well as the opposition. Using unusual formations before you are comfortable with how to play them correctly throws off your own team's focus. It is important to adequately practice any formation changes you wish to add to your team's options. This will help you understand which formation is best for your team and what to expect when you use it in the match.

43

Countering Unusual Doubles Formations

W hen a team tries an unusual formation against you, what should you do?

First, call time and discuss briefly with your partner how to best play against that formation. Most importantly, this is to make your partner aware the opponents are using an unusual formation, and so you can devise a plan. Next, decide what to expect from this formation and what you should do to make a definitive plan of action.

Teams that serve with the I-formations typically are vulnerable to a well-placed lob. Because the player up front in the I-formation is usually going to move to the left or the right, a strong shot up the middle is a good option, as that is the place they intend to leave to go left or right. When both players are back and you are returning deep to them, it is best to aim for the middle—between the players—to avoid providing them an angle to return back against you.

The key when facing an unusual formation is for you and your partner to stop and game-plan what your options are, and to plan to counter that particular formation as a team. While you may seldom face some of the formations, it is good to practice them and to have your friends use them against you.

44.

The Winning Mind-set for Game Tiebreakers

Tiebreakers are not like regular games in a set, where you can get behind or have your serve broken and have the luxury of a full game to get back into the game or set. The 7-point tiebreaker has a different dynamic that needs to be prepared for in your practice matches. Playing 7-point tiebreakers in place of regular sets can help you feel comfortable when you most need the mental confidence to play well.

Holding your serve or your team's serve is paramount in tiebreakers. First serves become paramount to get in play to set up your team, take the pressure off having to make a high-level second serve, and not allow the return team to attack your second serve. Game-plan how you want to attack your opponent's game, based on your experience in the set so far. Where have you been serving successfully? What have been the best return patterns up to this point? Who on the opposing team have you been attacking with most of your play?

Receiving and getting the ball in play in the tie-breaker is huge. Put the ball in play every chance you have. Every ball in play forces the other team to win a point or simply not make an error. This is always to your advantage.

Many players are not even aware of the rules in tiebreaker games concerning who serves, how many serves players get, what the rotations are on serving and switching sides, and who serves first starting the next set. The rules are the same for singles and doubles. When you learn how to play tiebreaking games, both mentally and technically, you'll have a major advantage over other teams.

45

10-Point Tiebreakers or Full Third Sets

|||||||||||||||||||||||||||||||||||||||||||||||||||||||||||||||||||||||||||||||||||||||

Before the match starts, the rules call for you to declare whether you intend to play a 10-point tiebreaker for the match or a full third set for the match. Usually, the home team declares what will occur. This generally applies to United States Tennis Association League matches as well. Tournaments will usually state what shall be played when you first enter the tournament.

My personal preference has always been to play a full third set. Not because I am a grinder but because my conditioning has always been an advantage for me, and I am an all-court player with options. I also feel I am not disposed to a lucky shot deciding the match. I prefer to practice matches using tiebreakers to force me to keep my focus and intensity.

If you are in great shape, a full third set can be to your advantage over an opponent who does not have your stamina. A grinder player, one who is fast and keeps the ball in play for several shots, would usually prefer to play a full third set for the match, as that is their strength.

While a 10-point tiebreaker is shorter in duration than the full third set, there can be a bit of luck involved in determining the winner. An unusual unforced error, a net-cord winner, an untimely gust of wind, or miss-hit shot can sometimes decide the match.

It is important that you practice playing 10-point tiebreakers, as the dynamics of the scoring is different than full set play. Knowing the rules is very important to being able to play with confidence. Know who starts the tiebreaker, when ends and servers rotate, when you switch after the first point or after 6 points, or whether you ever have to serve into the sun, if that was not your normal rotation. Knowing the rules will help avoid the confusion that can mess with your mental focus in a very critical situation.

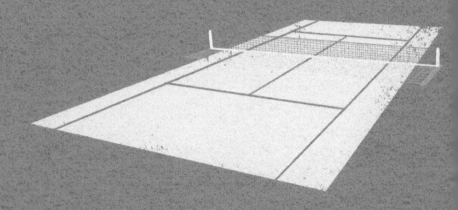

CHAPTER 5

POSTMATCH:
A TIME TO REFLECT

A typical response to a win is to enjoy the high without analyzing what happened before and during the match to allow such a positive result. Similarly, a typical response to a loss might be a completely negative evaluation with no real analysis of what the opponent did to affect your play or what mental challenges you faced that had an effect on your physical performance.

Postmatch performance evaluation is critical, but it should occur only once you have some downtime after the match is over and your emotions are slightly removed from the assessment. You need to allow time to come down from the emotional highs or lows of the match you just completed. Then, you can evaluate your performance with specific questions to ask yourself. This postmatch evaluation is best done with a coach. You need someone who can guide you with the correct questions to find the answers you need to learn from a loss or a win.

46

Identify Measurable Goals

In every tournament, regardless of the size of the draw, only one player or one team is crowned the champion; everyone else lost. Or did they? When you enter a tournament, you should have performance goals. These are goals that are measurable regardless of winning or losing a match. Initially they are best set with a coach who is working with your game and has a long-term approach to your performance.

Here are some examples of performance goals: 70 percent of my first serves in, keeping a positive attitude throughout the match, attacking any short balls, and going to the net or attempting to rally a specific number of balls before going for an aggressive shot. These types of goals can help you feel like a winner regardless of the match outcome. They are building blocks for future success and game planning. No one wins all the time if winning a tournament is their only goal.

"Tennis is a perfect combination of violent action taking place in an atmosphere of total tranquility."
—BILLIE JEAN KING

47

Evaluate the Performance, Not Just the Outcome

Looking at the results of a match as an outcome—I won or I lost—is not very helpful. What performance goals you set for yourself and how you performed these goals is the most important way to grow your game.

Examples of questions that help self-evaluate performance goals from a loss include the following:

- Did I get 60 to 70 percent of my first serves in?
- Did I manage my anger during the match?
- Did I hydrate on each of the changeovers?
- Did I set up patterns in the points?
- Did I manage the time between points to my advantage?

If you are able to answer yes to some of the performance goals you set, then you won! Match losses are inevitable and part of every player's career. If looked at positively, losses can provide opportunities to improve the most. Losing can help you become determined not to make the same mistakes again going forward.

When you win a match, it is easy to take for granted that you will continue to win. There is little desire to look at what made this performance a winning experience versus just wanting to enjoy the feeling of victory. However, even after a win it is important to evaluate your performance by asking the following questions:

What did I do today to manufacture the win?

What do I need to work on to improve my performance for the next event I play?

Was the win a product of my style of play versus their style of play, or was I able to overcome their style of play?

Learning from a match is the key to growth. If you choose to learn from your wins and losses, you are going forward. If you choose not to learn from your playing, you are moving backward. In tennis, your game seldom stays the same.

BILLIE JEAN KING

Billie Jean King brought tennis to the masses with her famous match against Bobby Riggs in the *Battle of the Sexes*, captured in a 2017 film starring Emma Stone and Steve Carell. Billie Jean would defeat Bobby and, in the process, expose tennis to the general public with all the publicity and television exposure the match received. Billie Jean and her husband, Larry King, would bring World Team Tennis to the tennis world in 1973. It features singles, doubles, and mixed doubles, with substitution of players allowed and team-based scoring.

Billie Jean won 39 Grand Slam titles—12 in singles, 16 in doubles, and 11 in mixed doubles. She was the first female to win $100,000 in prize money.

48

Five Additional Questions for Performance Self-Evaluation

||||||||||||||||||||||||||||||||||||||||||||||||||||||||||||||||||||||||

Here are some objective questions to help you better evaluate your performance:

1. What did the other player do well in this match against me?
2. What did I do well in this match against my opponent?
3. What were my opponent's weaknesses?
4. What areas of my game let me down?
5. If I could go out and replay this match, what would I do differently?

A realistic evaluation session using these questions can create a directed road map to improving your performances going forward. Results of the answers can provide direction for you and a coach to develop your strengths and shore up your weaknesses. This is how the pros on tour approach winning and losing on a weekly basis and game-plan for the future.

"Thinking about past points you lost only costs you future points."
—BILL TILDEN

49

Get an Outsider's Opinion

As the player, you are heavily emotionally engaged in the match. As a result, critical analysis is not easy for you. Tennis is easier from the sidelines! It is easy to see what should happen in situations while sitting in the bleachers watching a match. As a coach, I have seldom been wrong from the sidelines, and my choice of what to do in a game or set is spot on. However, my success rate goes down dramatically when I am on the court competing. We have all experienced a loss of perspective and experience when caught up in the throes of competition.

It is very helpful to have someone chart your match or, even better, have them video the match. The video will tell a different story than what you believed you were doing on the court. The pros usually sit down with a coach to review matches to improve their game, as athletes do in most sports. The analytics of serve percentages, shot selection, and length of points become more relevant when there is a realistic evaluation rather that an emotional review. In today's world there are many on-court cameras that can be mounted on a fence to capture your total match performance and the performance of your opponent. It is important to see what you did based upon what your opponent was doing to you.

As mentioned before, checking in with a coach or a friend who observed your performance can provide an objective critique of what really went on in your match. I am always so amazed by what actually happened versus my on-court evaluation of what happened.

50

Success in the Future

Focused practice helps you develop mental confidence, rituals, or patterns that you can repeat without conscious thought in match play. Developing positive and productive rituals in practice and before a match gives you options during the match to influence the outcome of your performance. Create pressure in practice by adjusting the scoring. This might include starting matches at 30-all and playing sets, playing with one serve only for a match, and winning 2 points if you win the point at the net. Altered scoring is a great way to practice under pressure.

Developing rituals for evaluating your performance and recovery patterns following performance is critical to future performance development. Match play analysis is important to proper evaluation of performance, using the five questions mentioned earlier in the book (page 139).

You need to be aware that progress is not a straight line. There will be many ups and downs in your tennis career. How you handle those cycles will help you grow in a positive direction with your game.

Many distractions may come from outside the game: family, work, injuries, etc. But the joy you experience can keep you coming out for more as life allows. Enjoy the journey, because you never know where it will take you.

Remember, at the end of the day, tennis is a game. How we improve and enjoy this game can be influenced by evaluation and focused practice and by challenging ourselves so we grow from where we are today to where we want to be in the future.

I have found that journaling my habits, my match results, and my private thoughts helps me see my journey, so I can make adjustments and keep improving.

It is my road map for success.

GLOSSARY

DYNAMIC STRETCHING. These are exercises that resemble movements that will be performed in a match. Dynamic stretching consists of elongating the muscle while in motion versus trying to lengthen a muscle while holding it in a static position. Dynamic stretching is best done during warm-up for a competition.

FULL THIRD SET. A full third set is played when two players of a team split sets, or each team has won a set. In these cases, the deciding set is a full third set; this will determine the winner of the match.

INTENSITY. Players often confuse intensity and tension. Intensity requires purpose and focus. Tension or "muscling" is not natural; it is gripping too tightly to play athletically. Tennis players bring intensity to the court when they play to avoid losing momentum and control of a match.

MATCH TIEBREAKER. When each player has won one set, the deciding factor is a match tiebreaker instead of playing a third set. The match goes to the first player to get to 10 points and is ahead by 2 points, such as 10-8.

NEURO-LINGUISTIC PROGRAMMING (NLP). This is a pragmatic school of thought that addresses the many aspects of the human experience. NLP is used in sports to create visual images and recall emotional and physical experiences from previous performances.

PLAY AGGRESSIVE. This term is often confused with trying to hit the ball harder. Instead, to play aggressive means to move forward to reduce an opponent's time to react to a shot you make. It can also make the player look at you instead of the ball, causing them to make an error. When you move forward toward the ball, you are playing aggressive.

PRESSURE POINT. In a match there is a point that can determine the outcome of a game, set, or match. There is no particular number when a pressure point occurs, but it is triggered by the previous point. For example, the deuce point will determine who has the ad point to win the game. Players think of the ad point as the pressure point, but it is the deuce point that triggers the ad point, a situation that is usually called the pressure point. Closing out a set or match when a player has the lead is a pressure point for the player with the lead.

PSYCHING OUT. This term refers to a player creating a mental distraction for their opponent that changes their opponent's thought processes and creates stress. It can be intentional or unintentional; in either case, it changes an opponent's mental focus. Causing an opponent to become angry or intimidated can cause them to lose focus on the match and fear the opponent or the outcome of a situation.

SPLIT STEP. This is a move a player makes just as their opponent begins their forward swing toward the ball. The receiving player would adjust their feet with a wide stance, so they're able to change the direction of their movement according to the direction of the ball. A split step could be one move or a series of small steps. A common analogy would be the move you would make with your feet while walking down the sidewalk to avoid bumping into another person coming in your direction.

TIEBREAKER. This term is used to describe how players decide who wins a set when the score reaches 6-all in a set. The set is decided by the player or team that reaches 7 points first and is ahead by 2 points, such as a score of 7-5.

UNUSUAL DOUBLES FORMATION. This refers to a doubles position other than the conventional four positions normally seen in doubles. They are used to change the momentum in a match or create a favorable formation against an opposing team. Unusual doubles formations can be used to hide a weakness in a game or to take advantage of a player's strength.

WATCHING VERSUS SEEING. Watching is an observational skill, while seeing is a focus skill. We watch television until we see a program we like. You might say to your coach, "I thought I was watching the ball." To which your coach responds, "You were. That is why you could not see it." Club players often mistake these two terms as being the same.

FURTHER READING

MATCH PLAY AND THE SPIN OF THE BALL by William T. Tilden. Written in 1948, this book is still relevant in the world of tennis today due to the author's strategy on strokes and mental skills. He was the master of the all-court game, handling pressure and showmanship. He was a champion well into his fifties; he also loved theater and working with actors and actresses. He was well versed in all aspects of the game including tactics and technique.

THE INNER GAME OF TENNIS by W. Timothy Gallwey. This is one of the first books ever to help club players learn how to quiet the mind to improve performance. Tim's approach was to simplify the mysterious nature of a player's mind so they could exhibit control and focus in competition.

PRESSURE IS A PRIVILEGE by Billie Jean King and Christine Brennan. Cowritten by one of the best pressure performance players of all time, Billie Jean looked forward to high-pressure situations as an opportunity to go beyond where she was each day. Some athletes love the moments of pressure in sports and life. This is when some players seem to perform their best—when results really matter.

WINNING UGLY by Brad Gilbert and Steve Jamison. Here's another classic for the club player. Olympic gold medalist Brad Gilbert explains how players can use their mental skills to take advantage of tactical situations and apply pressure to their opponents. You may be outskilled or outsized by an opponent, but there are ways you can unnerve them, psych them out, or find ways to play that limit their advantage. Brad is a noted television commentator and coach as well as a former tour player.

TENNIS INSIDE THE ZONE by Rob Polishook. I'm sure you have experienced playing in a unique place where performance is without conscious thought. It probably seemed like you were watching yourself perform. That moment is fleeting, so how do you find that zone again and stay in it for extended periods? Rob's book will show you how.

TENNIS: WINNING THE MENTAL MATCH by Allen Fox. This book outlines a common-sense approach you can use to improve your performance under pressure. A certified sports psychologist, professional player, and college coach, Allen was able to win on the pro tour using his skill set and mental understanding of the situations he faced. He passes those skills on to you in this book.

MIND GAMES: MENTAL FITNESS FOR TENNIS by Jason Whitmore and John Whitmore. Being physically fit can give you mental toughness, because you believe you have prepared to go longer and perform at a higher level than your opponent. This book helps provide that extra edge to maximize your athletic ability and improve your match play performance.

MOMENTUM: THE HIDDEN FORCE IN TENNIS by Alistair Higham and Cassie Bradley. In each match, there is a mystical momentum that constantly swings back and forth from one side of the court to the other. You can be up 4-1 or 5-2 and suddenly the momentum can switch to your opponent within a few points. A lot of it relates to managing your thoughts when you are ahead or when you are behind. This book will help you become aware of where this momentum lies, who has it, and how to manage it, ultimately enabling you to compete at a higher level.

TENNIS: WINNING THE MENTAL GAME by Robert Weinberg. With a PhD in psychology, Robert gives insights on how you can improve your tennis game using the power of the mind. So much of what we are able to do in physical performance relates to how well we manage our inner thoughts in the heat of competition.

THE INNER COACH by Dave Power and Dorothy Sheehy-Wieczorek. A former Association of Tennis Professionals men's tour player, Dave provides tips on how to coach yourself and offers ideas on how to grow by managing your mind during competition. On tour, players learn through experiences how to be their own coaches on the court and when winning and losing depends upon the next few points. David can give you insights into how you can be your own coach.

THE ZEN OF TENNIS: A WINNING WAY OF LIFE by Nancy Koran. Using principles of Eastern philosophy, Nancy provides tips on relaxing your focus to play your best game. The inner calmness learned from Zen masters can quiet the mind and allow the physical performance to happen without the mind's distractions at the wrong time.

MENTAL TOUGHNESS: WORKBOOK FOR TENNIS by Jorge Capestany. A club player's guide to analyzing your strengths and weaknesses. Using ideas from several mental coaches in tennis, Jorge gives the club player a workbook to access their mental and physical steps to improving and documenting their process. It is important to journal or have your success documented to go forward with your game or to look back and remind yourself of how you were able to get where you are today.

THINK TO WIN: THE STRATEGIC DIMENSION OF TENNIS by Allen Fox. Capitalizing on his years of experience on the pro tour, working with tour players, and coaching college players, Allen offers a practical approach to devcloping your mental skills to improve your performance on the court and in life. His common-sense approach to maximizing physical skills through understanding how to think in competition has improved the performance of many college and club players.

WHAT TO SAY WHEN YOU TALK TO YOUR SELF by Shad Helmstetter. It has been proven that we write our own destiny by how we communicate with our thoughts about ourselves. In essence, you become what you say to yourself. Learn how to improve the conversations you have with yourself to improve your life and performance.

THE TALENT CODE by Daniel Coyle. What makes certain groups of athletes, musicians, and performers evolve from what seems like anonymity to the highest level of performance? As Daniel's book outlines, our environment and those around us can affect whether we develop into high performers, even in unusual environmental settings. The author studies how these "pockets" of success develop and helps us replicate these success stories.

CONVERSATION WITH A ZEN TENNIS MASTER by Dr. Desmond Oon and Dr. Damien Lafont. Using the techniques of martial arts masters and a Zen-like approach to life can also improve your ability as a tennis player. The Eastern culture has long been proven as the grounds for strong mental performance in martial arts. Learn how you can use these concepts to improve your own wisdom about life and tennis.

THE EYE COACH WEBSITE created by Lenny Schloss, a former top 10 player in the world on the men's ATP tour. Lenny has a program for managing the mind by correct use of the eyes and keeping the head still during the point of contact. Go to howtoplaytennis.net for tips, drills, and how to use the program on the court or at home. How long you are able to keep your eyes still during and following a shot is a huge indicator of success on the court. It allows you to perform at your highest skill level. This can be learned, and is best seen in the stroke production of the great Roger Federer. Notice how long his head and eyes stay in one place well after the ball has been hit. This is one of the key secrets of all high-level sports performers.

INDEX

Tilden, Bill, 64, 140
Time confirmation, 23–24
Towels, 7
Travel details, 25–26
Tym, Bill, 14

U
"Ugly" tennis, 86

V
Video-recording, of matches,
141–142
Visualization, 19–20

W
Warming up, 31–32
Weaknesses
    of atypical doubles styles,
    97–100
    doubles teams, 120–122
    personal, 70–72
Williams, Serena, 106
Williams, Venus, 106
Windscreens, 66–67
Wristbands, 7

ACKNOWLEDGMENTS

My passion in life has been tennis. Being able to do all that tennis has allowed me to do comes only with the support of family and friends. My wife knows my passion for the game and all the related opportunities: speaking opportunities, traveling, new friends, reconnecting with old friends, and new challenges. These are the responsibilities of being available for club members and the duties required to be a director of tennis.

I admire the dedication my wife has demonstrated through her love of acting and the theater, all while still making time for family. Her positive approach to life is contagious, as is her love for our dogs.

My son inspires me to provide him with all the opportunities to experience life that I can. I have enjoyed exploring the world of tennis with him and watching him grow both as a tennis player and as a young man. I appreciate his help, his advice, and his guidance. I look forward to seeing who he will become in the coming years.

While my parents are gone, they gave me my foundation for life.

For all these people, I am grateful.

ABOUT THE AUTHOR

KEN DEHART is the director of tennis at the Silver Creek Valley Country Club in San Jose, California. He is a Professional Tennis Registry (PTR) Hall of Fame member, a PTR International Master Professional, two-time PTR International Pro of the Year, current member of the PTR Board of Directors, and former executive director of the PTR.

A USPTA Master Professional, Ken is also four-time USPTA Divisional Pro of the Year and three-time time winner of the Continuing Education Award for Career Development. Ken has been with Wilson for many years and serves as a Wilson Premier Advisory Staff and National Speaker. He is a USA High Performance Coach and an international speaker at the US Open, Wimbledon, and Australian Open Coaches Conferences. His topics include Drills and Games That Teach Strategy and Tactics, and Defeating the Monsters in Your Mind, among many others. Learn more about Ken and his topics on Facebook at Ken DeHart Tennis.